proxy

ISBN: 978-0-9823387-9-7

Cover, interior design, and typesetting by HR Hegnauer.
Selections from David Berlinski's *A Tour of the Calculus.* New York: Vintage Books, 1997.
Cover artwork © Julie Mehretu. *Vanescere*, 2007
    Ink and Acrylic on Canvas, 60 x 84 inches. Courtesy of Marian Goodman Gallery

Belladonna* is a reading and publication series that promotes the work of wom-
en writers who are adventurous, experimental, politically involved, multiform,
multi-cultural, multi-gendered, impossible to define, delicious to talk about,
unpredictable, & dangerous with language. Belladonna* is supported by funds
granted by the New York State Council on the Arts, the O Books Fund, and from
generous donations from our supporters. The book is also supported with a grant
from the Council of Literary Magazines and Presses and the Jerome Foundation.

State of the Arts

NYSCA

jerome
foundation

[clmp]

        Library of Congress Cataloging-in-Publication Data

            Doyle, R. Erica.
            [Poems. Selections]
            proxy / r. erica doyle.
                pages cm. -- (Belladonna* Series)
            Includes bibliographical references and index.
            Poems.
            ISBN 978-0-9823387-9-7
            I. Title.
            PS3604.O955P76 2013
            811'.6--dc23

                        2012044397

Distributed to the trade by   Also available directly through
Small Press Distribution   Belladonna*
1341 Seventh Street   925 Bergen Street, Suite 405
Berkeley, CA 94710   Brooklyn, NY 11238
www.SPDBooks.org   www.BelladonnaSeries.org

* deadly nightshade, a cardiac and respiratory stimulant, having purplish-red flowers
    and black berries.

proxy

r. erica doyle

BELLADONNA* 2013

The mathematician is inclined to minimize the details,
his intellectual movement retrograde
to that of the novelist or physician.
Revisiting the facts, the mathematician must resist
the tug of those very rich, very voluptuous descriptions of reality
that the novelist or physician might favor, dismissing them curtly
in favor of two austere abstractions —
change in position and change in time.
Under the mathematician's hands, the world contracts,
but it becomes more lucid.

— David Berlinski, *A Tour of the Calculus*

prologue

A limit is a fixed something toward which other somethings are tending.

— *A Tour of the Calculus*

In this fairytale, too, there is a castle. On a rise above a river. You enter in a cycle. The dew is come in words.

The grasp of the offered hand a falling in to spin, craned sequence, flashing before, as if. Curious, curious. The moment you knew everything — when she lifted her eyes from the plate. Her gaze was a solar wind, stripping. *All the years I* — The horse of your heart.

You couldn't stop writing her. Etched the letters along your ribs. Painted subway tiles with a bloodied finger. A small underground paper proclaimed the nonsense. *I'm just as confused as the next person,* you said. Ridiculous.

She is the gape of a second. A glyph you remembered how to read. The other lovers rattle their sabers. They don't see WHAT. She's not really THAT. It's all a cumulus din you wade around in when she leaves for years. Her words, a dry arroyo. It is all an ice pack, Novocain, delirium tremens, the haze left after a high fever. Until she comes back.

You hope to perform an autopsy. The dead and the nagging questions. The mountain you retreat to has a dirt road with a stream across it. When it's dark, it's really dark, so you're glad she's come. Her words, a pregnant creek. You have some feeling in your right molar. Each timber of the porch a clarified geometer. The gleam of white you find while walking the dog is quartz — the mountain's flush with it — and each and every red dusted stone yields shining flesh. You've come to do an autopsy and at the first excision found a beating heart.

Is seven such a lucky number? Now you've changed enough to be cynical. After seven years, you've regenerated every cell in your body. After seven years, there's some new constellation in your house of damage. After seven years, you've fucked enough women to know better. After seven years, the slant of her eyes tilts your beautiful, wavering house, complete with wife and dog, into the chasm behind the curtain.

palimpsest

A [ ] is thrown into the air. At its extremities it changes its behavior.

Something so simple as a [ ] in flight
has acquired a tripartite aspect,
a critical point
lying between points marking its regular behavior.

— *A Tour of the Calculus*

You are a third generation beast in a first generation world of open legs.

You were six when you read your mother's Marquis de Sade. It explained so much about things in the house. Kama Sutra at seven, but you remained unimpressed. Likewise, at eight, by the flaccid illustrations in *The Joy of Sex*. Yet, the paintings of Shoji at nine, kimonos parted over thick white penises, the arc of them shining into pleated vulvas.

You talk to them first, pay close attention to details, are interested and easily amused. Women like that. Always a voracious reader, you turn their pages, memorize the deep structure of their grammar, their adjectival clauses. A question in private that puts them off guard. Women are so polite. So crisscrossed with borders. Sometimes it's like stealing. Taking something you don't really want just to. Get away with it. Sometimes you tell them you love them. Sometimes, not often, this is true.

You hold back enough to keep them curious. Women like that. Wounded enough to be salvageable. Women like that, too. Fixing things. Take in the broken wing you drag like a decoy.

You fuck artfully, are disappointed by graceless fumblings. You give them one more chance, just to placate your horrified friends. To say, I fucked her twice, avoid the one-night-stand hisses. Not that the PR helps your reputation or your sex life. Some things do not improve with time.

You are hungry. Each one tastes different. Lavish tongue wherever they push your mouth. Creases slick with sweat and hair and the particular liquid of an armpit. You are not clean. You are not fresh. You are not pleased with extended foreplay. You want the fuck. Your hands as full of cunt as the stretch can dare, the edge of pain and fear. Their screams delicious bells pealing, small large rough soft hands grabbing.

Sometimes you make an offering of yourself. They think they take and you open wide to swallow them whole.

You are not generous.

One holds herself aloft and fucks you dry with the thick black cock. Unrelenting, fucks your ass, slathers the lube and turns you over again.

And again, you assume.

One pushes your fist away. You rewind and tease until she begs, kneels ass like a harvest moon. A difficult position, blood spilling from your wrist.

You do not make promises.

One stumbles in the shower, gasps choking on the water full in a mouth turned away from you, a tongue you've bitten for hours.

You do not plan to keep.

One you coax and beg and cajole. She doesn't say yes but she doesn't say no. You suck her asshole until her cunt is wet and fuck her with your tongue until she sighs.

You are not conjunctive—

One sits on your cock while you think about her boyfriend.

You are perfect.

One cries from her urethra while you suck her clit.

You are dangerous.

One's anus spirals out around your finger.

You are unapologetic.

One's youth gives beneath your knee, crisp indentations.

You are born.

When you can't fuck hunger makes you walk the streets alone and weep. If the moon is full your womb is an aching crater. The doctor says your hormones are fucked up. She wants you to take the pill to stabilize them. They make you feel pregnant and bitter and you won't stop smoking. You quit taking them though it means you will get cancer. The eggs struggle against the membrane and wait to be let out, die and decay there, festering cysts. On the sonogram, your ovaries like asteroids against the tulips of your fallopian tubes.

When you can't fuck you write about not fucking. You plan the next escapade, have dreams where you hook up with blue-eyed Australian men. You kiss women young enough to be your daughters, masturbate several times a day and get no work done.

Your friends say that this is good for you, that you need to stop fucking so much. That if you do it less you will think about it less. They are lying as usual. You think they are jealous of how you feed, how they repress their own gluttony. You think of sins, of church, of priests, of how the hood of the clitoris is like a nave of a cathedral.

You are not penitent.

When you haven't fucked for long enough you make bad fuck judgments. You fuck a lawyer who has never fucked a woman before. "Women are so kind," says the virgin. "Women are sensitive and caring." Her hope is a virus. You say nothing. She makes good rum cake and wants to watch TV. You fuck her tiny cunt with three fingers while you patiently suck her clit. You are unceremonious. You disabuse.

You fuck your best friend the night before your father's funeral.

You fuck your ex's best friend the week before you get back together with your ex.

You fall in love.

You fall in love with a star in a different constellation, city, state, relationship. Her lovers have good credit and dark hair. She meets you in the back room of your cunt. You fuck her in the armchair before the fireplace when her lover is away, pull down the laces of her mouth and shove your hand into the bruised cuff of her cunt. Her face is a quick flush of heat, lips purple from your teeth. You blind, bind, beat. Her geography wears at your nipples. You map her in reticent bodies, know a crystal glass by how it sings beneath your moistened fingers.

You lend money. When you are not fucking, your generosity knows no bounds. When you have no more money, you share your food. When you have no more food, you give good advice. Everyone tells you you should be a therapist.

You have been lying since you were six. The Marquis de Sade was all about presentation. Your origin is a story your mother used to quell the troops. Your luteinizing hormone will not release the eggs. Cunt judgment. The gynecologist laughed. You were eighteen years old and she thought your dickless state was a joke. You are not a joke and you have your own dicks. You refuse to make love. Take the consumptive tunnel and give it fuck. The edge of the tub, the arm of the sofa, your brother's rocking horse, fruit, vegetables, tongues, fists, nipples, fingers, toes, toothbrushes, bottles, candles, handles, plastic, porcelain, silicone, glass.

You are not injured. You are not healing. You are taking it lying down.

proxy

Each curve is what it is and not some other thing

and so a specific record and a particular expression
of how time passes *now* and how space changes *here*.

— *A Tour of the Calculus*

The entries are usually in black. This entry is painted in blue. Paint head. Everyone trying on a new voice for size. In separate accounts, a corridor. Dust and rank, humid echo. Your footsteps carry here. You weave among stone columns, erected to an open sky. Walls nonetheless. Across the plaza, Thoth. Ausar. Auset. Horus. Thoth's plume extends from a point perpendicular to his navel. If you dared, you'd touch it. You cannot read his face. *My cartouche is open*, you tell him. His dull eyes regard eternity with a desert hound's acuity. *My heart is a pendant*, you tell him.

You are wandering the corridors of Never and If Only. The doors are painted on the walls, a pantheon of trompe l'oeil. You draw your hand along cool plaster. Light emanates from the stones on the floor. Nut passes the sun through her anus. Nothing opens here. Beneath your feet, lost alabaster gleams.

The next thing is semiotic and eternal. Your pen has dried. You're driving toward fanaticism. You're visiting the Intrepid and pretending you're the captain. You're going to nuclear bomb something beautiful. You will leave no child behind. You are a naturally occurring phenomenon, a cyclone, a printer's gasp.

Are we — in the face of the storm the ex-lover's coattails flutter like eyelids. One is unbattened. Her irises are enormous shining platters. On each, a liquid serving. Soup, she likes soup. You are exiled in the land of terrible choices. You are a heathen who does not know what priority means. *Her hands are my priority.* *She* has always been first in all things, what you were before, are becoming. Your trope. *Priority*, you lie. You say you do not know. *I. Will. Have. To. See.*

Is it evil to rend so. Shrug without hesitation or apology. The ex-lover's eyes fill with tears. Darken. Raw fish sticks at the back of your throat. *Best*, she crumbles. The ex-lover is so young, you think, foolish, forget anything wise.

Dash and crinkle and stomp. The news lays in pieces on the floor. She creeps barefoot and bleeding, her penance insufficient. She calls from the bath. *We've spun and spun, and now the dizziness.*

Fall, you say—

Fall. Be still and counter the trick you've played on your ears. Time is draped across the door. She calls. You made a horrible mistake. Between you the golden thread shines. It's made of blood and hope. You drag yourself along its solid length.

Your bed is the frosty garden October mornings she's gone. A light is flashing somewhere. A disembodied voice announces textual desire. In your mind you hear her call for water.

If her writing were more precise, you'd read her more. In the same vein, even. You'd be more glamorous on the other side, where beauty and romance reside. What she writes you is genius, but you had to delete it, drag it to the trash, it was secret. Concede defeat. Code deranged angels. Deny her. *This is not me. I wrote it but it is not from me.* If she sends the message three ways you'll get it in tripartite stew — all virtual, electronical, in a Victorian instant message or a voicemail from the Marquis de Sade. An IM from your mother covers hers, bleeping. About Thanksgiving. Another thicket. There are deer in the woods behind your mother's house. You lurk behind her text box.

If she were any closer, you'd eat her for dinner. As it is, you're starving. And not. You weather this all with seeming good humor. Write notes to amuse yourself. You have become too earnest, trying so hard to mean something important. Watch the drain and hear your stomach growl. *Negroes make me hungry, too*, she says. You need an explanation but say nothing to this boastful non sequitur. You want to amuse her with your bones.

Half asleep you stumble from train to train and doze embracing your backpack. The oldest stations smell the best. The elevator at 168th is silent with bodies and Catholic school uniforms. Sleepy children trail from brisk arms. A million empty seats. The sky is easy today. In Marble Hill, the buildings sit brickly on small ridges, slight rising. The sun places a little morning in each pale window, sweet water, purple orange nectar.

In the train on the way to see her you fall into a deep sleep, pass through forests of cool brown pillars, feel the rumbling in your bones. Off track. En route. Hurtling. In the dream, head lamps, ever oncoming. The light of day waiting above. The doors open, singing.

At the Soho exit, you skulk, unleashed. Resist, passive. A movie star passes you, much shorter than the screen. You nod knowingly at passersby. There is a squeaking in your hand.

This time you were only trying to put her to sleep but she wouldn't behave. You shot so many horses from under her but she would not rest. You let her think that would be it, that she wouldn't have given you her precious insides. On the edge of grovel and granted, you sat astride her back and tied her hands. This tender captaincy, the grainy stash, this hardened fossiter under her eyes. You're turning the equator and groping along an edge to the crisp teeth perched on her purple lips, hiding your treasure, and seek.

phasedown

In the single efflorescent instrument of a differential equation
the particular is seen as an aspect of the general
and the general seen as an aspect of the particular.

— *A Tour of the Calculus*

Now you play at illusions. Storm clouds rumble above her house. *I think we should be friends, for just—.* If any of that mattered, you'd have already gnawed off your leg. You are refuge at the end of a dangerous path. The navy put microbes on the boots of colored men, to mimic the tracking of deadly viruses. The chemical warfare heats up. Over dinner with your brother, he coughs. It sounds like her on the phone, afterwards. Dragging the infestations, everyone, dragging.

You watch the men march on television. She is a letter in the envelope of your body. A general with your father's mouth sputters over documents. Something about obstruction and leaning. You crease. She unfolds. The bold paragraph in the dimple of her back is blue.

She is here but you can't see her. It's another blank mirror, an atom thumb. Between seats the heads spill in cracks — silent, nodding. She runs by the aisle, you make excuses, run after. You cannot find her. You search the labyrinthine basement, a wall that curves whitely. You run your hand along, pursuing space the curvature of blank longing. You run up the stairs, two at a time, outside to where a man freezes and smokes a cigarette or is it an icicle, or is it the bicycle your brother left in the shed, pouring from his face, the past in his cheeks, something green and rusting, humid, a nightmare, the one in which you, breathless, re-enter the hall and sit too many rows behind her and her girlfriend.

Your mother sits in the house. She eats marriage. No she doesn't. That's a lie. You wish she would be that TV show you run in your mind, but she is a scented hair, a bulging torso where you once lived. How did that body sustain you, did you feed like this, hidden at first, the wrong pregnancy, was anything worth this entirely. Between a focus of nose and eye, the sofa where she sits and sits and sits. You are burned. It's all buried. If there were a dreaming, here it would begin, even between arch. If thunder were a vowel, this is the lip it would occupy.

You are a child pulling your lips back from your teeth in the mirror. Two fingers deep along the side of your cheeks and pull, pull, pull until you see the bones of your face, the skull that lurks behind your eyes.

You're dying. Doesn't everybody know it.

Everything the same terrible color.

Gather in her breasts like sails. Like nets and draw deep. The hand pumps between. A link to turning inside out.

All the displaced lust in the world would not pacify this quest. The fist in the center of your chest is turning. Everything behind it is wet and begging. Your ears pop in the tunnel. Fragrances of sound emerge dully. Postulate, postulate, gratiating consciousness. Around the fist the scar tissue thickens. You were born with that wound. It's getting deeper.

They make all the usual gestures but you can't reciprocate. Your gills flap feebly in the eaves. This mouth, that mouth humming a stillborn melody. Bees fall from your lips.

In the white house there is a terrace on top of the garage. The shutters are red, baleful eyes. You tell time by the muezzin. At the end of the journey there's some kind of danger. You cover your hair and walk to the beach. Old women grip the ends of their safsaris in their teeth. After two greasy pastries, you watch the boys tear their shirts off and race into the Mediterranean. As if in a thousand broken thermometers. Pretty brown boys and mercury. They will not die from it. The same reassurances. *This may just pinch a little bit. You're going to feel some stinging. Now this might burn for a second. This might hurt but it won't kill you.* Dogs and pine trees. Pebble after pebble.

You heard some news and knelt. You heard some news and laughed. You heard some news and your skin cracked. You heard some news and your chest crashed. You heard some news and bit blood. She says, *No, no, no* and *no.* Says, *Yet, yet, yet* and *yet.* In another frequency, opposite notes demand a scale.

Could the Jerome Street reservoir hold the slate sky any closer than desire? A pigeon the color of dried blood struts and dips. Black squirrels with ochre bellies inquire about nothing. She builds with someone else in a home between here and there. Your belly churns with chocolate nicotine. A girl shouts at the steam-covered glass in a deli, *The food is breathing! I'm getting outta here.* What has gnawed at bones flagellates.

A fine quill. A computer screen. A blinking cursor winks its eye. The beckoning is pink between your teeth. The moan of a street sweeper. Pigeons growl atop dead air conditioner. Sound permutates. The same sigh of your mouth on flesh.

You graph the words only after she has spoken. Open the door and they come tumbling out. *Voice, voice,* you are calling. Are you her puppet, or a channel? When she is silent, a dead volcano, you too, sleep. Numb up. The anesthesia of her absence. Just a call — *I'm prattling* — rattles your bones awake.

You're crying on the phone to anyone who will listen. *My heart is a blister,* you croak. They all hang up. Dial tones greet your frozen ears. Wandering the elevated platforms of the outer boroughs, old women clutching Christmas packages watch you with remorse. Or so you perceive. The sky has the same deep blank as the dial tone.

petroglyph

The world remains forever more various

than the symbols used to contain it.

— *A Tour of the Calculus*

After you, your ex-lovers seem to fall into more promising arrangements. Ba-dum, they find the perfect one they thought you were, with your salmon twisting. Each time, you smile on the phone, murmur, *Of course*, or *Guaranteed*. Sometimes you meet them for coffee uptown, receive cooing emails of their children. You run into your friends on the street. Your ex begs goodbye, her husband is waiting. Your friends appreciate her ass, ask, *Were you two ever together?* You say, *No, not really.*

Months down the weave of this pretty narrative. They *ooh* and *aah* and you call, bleeding. Her tongue is an ice tray. *Clink clink* spill her words into your head. They melt somewhere in the middle of your chest.

Everything she's given you has expired. The lotion from Provence. The tangerine bath gel. Empty. Cleaning to see this gleam. Leave enough filth to make a difference. On a ledge, cells and cells of hunger.

The night your chest exploded, you got a boy to take your mind off. Unlike the other boys you'd loved, you fucked this one. Anything to fill the hole she'd left. Took him inside to push everything else out. In the daylight the apartment smelled of latex and bitter sweat and a black hole gaped at the corner of the bed. You sent him on his way. The easy anonymity of straight people — there are so many of them. He blearily offered a movie as you pushed him out the door. She doesn't answer.

She's throwing telephones at cars, in cars, on bars. The voice is a wall between your skin and her will. She stands you up once, twice, until you stop counting and go slack in the current. Your teeth remain on the edge of the furious web, chew and chewing closer. Blistered gums and wet cunts, mustard colored dream eyes.

In the morning of a night the lover has not called. The lips you thirst for on another's neck. Next to a familiar body, a chasm grows in the mattress. No turning back the back you've turned to covet a ghost. Your heart a black water tank waiting behind the house for a drought that never comes. You took her silence for assurances. Feverish manacles.

The night is longer than a star's crossing, and in it, you sink.

Darting flies leave red blotches the size of a quarter. A man sleeps wrapped inside a palm frond on the side of a dusty road. Cows bawl all night long for their masters. The birds wake you with their cries. Even the sea heaves with sighs. All is calling. Will you leave this dengue plateau? The hills of Laventille wither beneath a moon that beats back the darkness of the plain. Shadows call her name to a lightening sky. Against hope and the force of the sea you weave her face in the sand, the mask memory leaves you.

You toss your words again and again into the fountain, where the letters glimmer like coins. The year bears the stretch marks of how you woke from arms that held you safe and sleeping. Your eyes no longer close. The stars have claimed you. In the room, love sleeps where you've left it to follow crumbs that vultures covet. Tree crabs scuttle beneath your groping fingers. Boas curl bones in the forks of branches.

A leatherback confused by streetlights, you hover in the shadows. The golden thread that pulled from your diaphragm ends in frayed tangles. In your chest the burning begins. The compass points west. The sun sets in the north. If only your hands did not tremble so, here, if only you could keep the skin from sloughing off your chest in sheets, take your own hand, release the blade that cuts your palm, and walk into the day.

Life has only this to offer: itself and death. You sip the sweat of a limb, pursue the sanctum of any thigh, to bring yourself back from the edge. Each pulse in a cervix, clemency; an arc from the noose; a dulling liqueur. Swimming across mountains of opiate breast and pelvis. All the while your tongue barks how vile you are, how vile.

Across these patient landscapes, mines. In the arch of a nostril, poison. Behind the ribs, rope. Oblivion beneath their eyes. Skin to skin, you hold those lovers from your broken rooms. When you thought you swallowed, you were consumed. Where the bodies fall away, mirrored walls, circle of glass. Images mouthing beneath dilated pupils to where there is no echo.

The Sahara is a page. A desert so vast it could only be named "desert." The thing itself, and the idea of it, and all deserts after it named what kind of facsimile. Gobi. Sinai. You climb the hills strewn with rocks behind Mohammed, named like the desert, and the night is falling and donkey brays at your side, irritable. Ali hits it with a pipe that whistles against its dusky hide. Your Mary Janes are stained with pee and dust. Your feet push thickly at the half moon and ankle. The diplomat doesn't care about the moon rising, or the fact that you have peed on your own feet out here. She is trying to keep her knee from breaking. She is pushing on, ahead of you, not looking back, caught up in it was all her own idea. You stumble and your head snaps back as the Milky Way cascades into your mouth.

The call collapses. The year is birthed. A coward to tell you what you already knew. *I can't.* The night the rails called and the front of train slamming to sleep. The dull roar of your chest. The horse there. Quilt of anger. As the fires burned on the river, the smoke curled around her face turned back to you, singing elemental. In that place, this fall, you walk alone as the music hums beneath the bridges and the three rivers burn together in the night.

Ah, but it's beautiful, you say. And, *You should walk with me*. Silken belly. Cumulus layers shelve stratocumulus and far, far about. The nimbus of her hair. Each melted emerald eye an ember bereft. The fading shore from the prow of a boat. Your mother waving goodbye.

r. erica doyle was born in Brooklyn to Trinidadian immigrant parents, and has lived in Washington, DC, Farmington, Connecticut and La Marsa, Tunisia. Her work has been anthologized in *Best American Poetry, Our Caribbean: A Gathering of Gay and Lesbian Writing from the Antilles, Gumbo: A Celebration of African American Writing, Bum Rush the Page: A Def Poetry Jam, Gathering Ground: A Reader Celebrating Cave Canem's First Decade* and *Voices Rising: Celebrating 20 Years of Black Lesbian, Gay, Bisexual and Transgender Writing.* Her poetry and fiction appear in various journals, including *Ploughshares, Callaloo, Bloom, From the Fishouse, Blithe House Quarterly* and *Sinister Wisdom.*

Her articles and reviews have appeared in *Ms. Magazine, Black Issues Book Review* and on the *Best American Poetry* and *Futurepoem* blogs. She has received grants and awards from the Hurston/Wright Foundation, the Astraea Lesbian Writers Fund, the DC Commission on the Arts and Humanities, the Humanities Council of DC and Poets and Writers, and she was a New York Foundation for the Arts Poetry Fellow. Erica is also a fellow of Cave Canem: A Workshop and Retreat for Black Writers.

In addition, she has read her work at the Kennedy Center, the National Black Arts Festival, Joe's Pub, the Nuyorican, the Calabash International Literary Festival in Jamaica, WI and various colleges and universities. Erica received her MFA in Poetry from The New School, and lives in New York City, where she is an administrator in the NYC public schools and facilitates Tongues Afire: A Free Creative Writing Workshop for queer women and trans and gender non-conforming people of color.

Grateful acknowledgment is made to the following publications in which some of these poems have appeared:

Best Black Women's Erotica 2: "palimpsest"

Belladonna*: "phasedown"

fishouse: "penitent," "purdah," and "pommerac"

Parts of "petroglyph" were commissioned by the Composers Collaborative inc for the Non Sequitur Festival and performed with music by composer Joshua Fried at the Flea Theater, New York, NY; parts of "petroglyph" were also commissioned and performed for the Transmodern Performance Festival with visual artist and sound designer Torkwase Dyson at the G-Spot in Baltimore, MD.

The author would also like to thank the Cave Canem Foundation, the New York Foundation for the Arts and the Astraea Lesbian Foundation for the grants and time during which this book sought its genesis and was completed.

Grateful acknowledgement is made to my family, both chosen and gifted, for the unconditional love and support without which none of this work is possible, and the many collectives—Belladonna*, Fire & Ink, Tongues Afire, Black Took, New York Writers Coalition, Audre Lorde Project—that help it breathe.

green press
INITIATIVE

Belladonna Books is committed to preserving ancient forests and natural resources. We elected to print this title on 30% postconsumer recycled paper, processed chlorine-free. As a result, we have saved:

1 Tree (40' tall and 6-8" diameter)
1 Million BTUs of Total Energy
114 Pounds of Greenhouse Gases
618 Gallons of Wastewater
42 Pounds of Solid Waste

Belladonna Books made this paper choice because our printer, Thomson-Shore, Inc., is a member of Green Press Initiative, a nonprofit program dedicated to supporting authors, publishers, and suppliers in their efforts to reduce their use of fiber obtained from endangered forests.

For more information, visit www.greenpressinitiative.org

Environmental impact estimates were made using the Environmental Defense Paper Calculator. For more information visit: www.edf.org/papercalculator